EAST ENTRANCE / SVENSSON '81

SKETCH STUDIES L.D. '81
OF RESTAURANT DETAILS

Opryland Hotel
NASHVILLE

The Story of
AN AMERICAN CLASSIC

Photography by Robin Hood and Dean Dixon
History by James A. Crutchfield

Feature Text by Barry Parker and Carolyn Mitchell

Parker Hood
Press

OPRYLAND HOTEL: NASHVILLE
The Story Of An American Classic

For information, contact: Director of Special Promotions, Opryland Hotel,
2800 Opryland Drive, Nashville, TN 37214; phone: 615/889-1000; or:
Parker Hood Press, Inc., 340 Crest Terrace Drive, Chattanooga, TN 37404;
phone: 800/563-1235

Library of Congress Control Number: 00-091417
ISBN 0-9645704-4-0

Designed by Robertson Design, Inc., Brentwood, Tennessee
Separations by Color Systems, Inc., Nashville, Tennessee
Printed in Hong Kong through Asia Pacific Offset, Inc.
Published by Parker Hood Press, Inc., Chattanooga, Tennessee

FIRST EDITION

PREVIOUS PAGE: SIGNATURE FLAG AND ROOFLINE OF THE
    OPRYLAND HOTEL

THIS SPREAD: MAGNOLIA ENTRANCE, OPRYLAND HOTEL

FOLLOWING SPREAD: THE GENERAL JACKSON PLIES THE
    CUMBERLAND RIVER

This book is dedicated to

Jack Vaughn

His pioneering vision and pursuit of excellence
created one of the world's greatest hotels.
His inspirational leadership was guided by the belief that
"a hotel is only as great as its employees allow it to be."

INTRODUCTION

I love the Opryland Hotel. If you are not a hotelier, that may sound odd. But like many of my colleagues at other classic hotels, I'm passionate about excellence in hotels and quality guest service, and what better way to illustrate this passion than to introduce you to the Opryland Hotel.

Some hotels actually have personalities. The Opryland Hotel definitely does. I have known this hotel for more than two decades, and now I have the privilege of serving as its president. For many reasons, I wanted its story told, and that is the purpose of this book.

My early encounters with the Opryland Hotel were as a consultant. The management hired me to visit the facility, checking rooms to compare service levels against standards, dining in its restaurants, and interacting with the staff, all done anonymously. I had worked for other hotel companies, but had never seen or experienced service, atmosphere and amenities comparable to that of the Opryland Hotel.

Its size and grandeur are what most people notice first. Our success in growth has been unparalleled, from 600 rooms originally, to 2,884 today, and with public and meeting spaces like no other hotel. While the size of the hotel gets people's attention initially, it's the friendliness of our team members that our guests say creates memories for a lifetime.

The hotel itself is only bricks and mortar, beds and china, computers and luggage tags. People — team members, entertainers, managers, and guests — make the hotel come alive, and that is what I love. When looking at all the grandeur and working with and associating with these people, I feel great passion, pride, excitement and joy.

The Opryland Hotel has produced legends in the hotel industry, and a gentleman named Jack Vaughn stands at the top of that list. He helped establish a tradition of excellence at this hotel and nurtured it for more than two decades. I wanted the many traditions and accomplishments of the hotel to be documented in this book. My goal, and the goal of every team member, is to carry on this proud tradition.

I hope you enjoy the story.

Jack L. Gaines

President, Opryland Hotel and Attractions

n a bright spring day in 1968, Irving Waugh, president of WSM radio and television in Nashville, walked into the home office of WSM's parent corporation, the National Life and Accident Insurance Company. To Waugh it was like a trip home, since WSM, owner of the world-famous Grand Ole Opry, had maintained offices in the National Life building in downtown Nashville from the day of its first broadcast in 1925. By 1966, however, WSM's rapidly expanding operations had outgrown their space and relocated to new quarters west of the city.

National Life's Finance Committee was meeting that day, and Waugh had been invited to appear before the group to present an idea he had been toying with for some time. Before he took the elevator to the meeting, however, he stopped by the office of his friend, Valentine W. Smith, an assistant vice president in National Life's Mortgage Loan Department. Smith listened intently as Waugh described his proposal to create a musical theme park in Nashville. When Waugh was through, Val Smith smiled broadly and told his friend he thought it was a superb concept and wished him every success with his presentation.

As the elevator doors opened to the 10th floor, Waugh stepped into the handsome lobby of the National Life executive suites. While awaiting the committee's summons, the former NBC journalist reviewed two highly positive considerations that favored his proposal. The first was that insurance companies constantly search for safe, yet lucrative, investment opportunities. Wise investments, whether in real estate, stocks and bonds, or unique projects like the one Waugh was about to present, are a major source of an insurance company's income. And, of the 1,700 life insurance companies operating in the United States and Canada in 1968, National Life had positioned itself among the nation's top 20, with total assets of nearly $1.5 billion and insurance in force of more than $9 billion.

Waugh's second selling point was the growing appeal of theme parks. Since opening in Anaheim, California, in 1955, Disneyland had maintained a virtual monopoly on the concept of combining rides, restaurants, shops and entertainment around a central theme, in its case, the cartoon characters created by Walt Disney. For 13 years, the unique park had lured tens of thousands of visitors through its gates every week. Now, as the decade of the 1960s drew to a close, other parks were being visualized, including a new one by the Disney people to be built near Orlando, Florida.

Waugh made his presentation to the National Life Finance Committee that day in 1968, emphasizing his recommendation that the park be a venture of both WSM and National Life. The facility's theme would be a celebration of American music—not just country, for which Nashville was already internationally recognized, but all varieties of music. Besides offering rides, shops and other attractions, the park would feature original musical programs and live stage shows. Forty-five minutes after catching the elevator to the 10th floor, a beaming Waugh stopped back by Smith's office and informed him the committee not only liked his idea, but its members had approved a full-blown feasibility study to judge its merits.

The study was conducted by Economic Research Associates of Los Angeles. ERA's report to National Life

GEORGE D. HAY, MANAGER OF PIONEER NASHVILLE RADIO STATION WSM, LAUNCHED THE GRAND OLE OPRY, WHICH NBC CARRIED NATIONWIDE.

NATIONAL LIFE AND ACCIDENT INSURANCE COMPANY'S HOME OFFICE WAS DECORATED FOR A VISIT BY PRESIDENT FRANKLIN ROOSEVELT TO NASHVILLE IN 1934.

recommended construction of the proposed theme park, carried out in three phases: the park proper; a new, in-the-park Grand Ole Opry House to replace the decaying Ryman Auditorium in downtown Nashville; and Oprytown, a mini-village that would contain offices, commercial shops, restaurants and a 200-room motel. Shortly after the feasibility study was reviewed by all concerned, National Life approval was given for land acquisition and construction of Waugh's theme park, to be called Opryland USA. Smith was charged with finding a suitable site for the $31 million complex.

1 8 5 0

As the Cumberland River meanders through Middle Tennessee, it forms a series of large elbows. One of these is called Pennington Bend, named for John Pennington, an early settler who, by 1850,

Nashville Banner.

WSM Radio Section		WSM Radio Section

VOL. L. No. 178   NASHVILLE, TENN., SUNDAY OCTOBER 4, 1925.   D   DAILY 3c—SUNDAY 5c

ANNOUNCING OPENING OF WSM

MONDAY NIGHT
(October 5th)
Continuous Program
From 7 P. M. to 2 A. M.

WSM Completed Dream of National Life Insurance Company

WSM, super-power 1,000-watt radio broadcasting station, now being dedicated to Nashville, the home city of The National Life & Accident Insurance Co., is the completed dream of the big insurance company's executives, who when planning the erection of The National's beautiful home building, included in their plans the erection of one of the finest broadcasting stations the country affords.

Following the completion of The National Building, first steps were taken toward the building of the powerful station. Vice-President E. W. Craig (himself an ardent radio fan) was commissioned to begin the task of gathering together the best ideas of the radio world. The National Company earnestly devoted time and study to radio's advantages as exemplified by leading broadcasting stations in the United States, and many trips were made during the past year by Mr. Craig. Consultations were held with radio experts over the country, and the best ideas of them all were collected for the purpose of incorporating them in the station that Nashville can proudly boast of as one of the very finest, equaled by only one other Southern station, and stronger than eighty-five per cent of all broadcasting stations in the United States.

Many obstacles had to be overcome before a class B wave length could be secured. As there are no exclusive Class B wave lengths obtainable, through the courtesy and co-operation of Dr. James D. Vaughan, owner and operator of station WOAN, a class B station operating on 282.8 meters, at Lawrenceburg, Tenn., arrangement was made by which station WSM could divide time on the air. This proved to be a very fortunate arrangement, as a class B wave length is considered to be the highest class functioning under a standard set by the Department of Commerce at Washington.

Among the many difficult tasks encountered by The National's scouts was the working out of details in connection with the remote control system. This system was adapted for use by WSM, after investigation upon investigation had been made as to its practibility. The remote control system was chosen for increased efficiency and it is said to be the practice of the most recent radio installations.

Next to be considered was the selection of a suitable site for the giant towers and radio machinery. This had to be found in a section where water pressure is good and a three-phase electric current could be had, also the location had to be available for four private telephone circuits, thus the selection on Fifteenth avenue, south, near Ward-Belmont.

After much thought and toil all of the apparently insurmountable difficulties were mastered and as a result the very latest and most perfect transmitting equipment, one which will carry to the world the worthy presentation of all that Nashville stands for, is now being placed at the disposal of the capital city's as well as the state's best talent by an Insurance Company that has already made her home city famous.

The National Life & Accident Insurance Co.'s Field Force of more than 2,500 working in as many cities and towns in twenty-one states who have never faltered in their efforts to aid in building what is now known as one of America's strongest Life Insurance Companies, are elated over the great station and they are telling thousands daily of the station that is destined to put Nashville on the International Radio Map.

Western Electric Company to Install Loud Speakers for Public

Due to the limited number of persons able to be accommodated in WSM's auditorium, the station regrets that it cannot invite the general public to be present at the studio on opening night, October 5, but in order that those who have no receiving sets who desire to hear the program can do so, the Western Electric Company will install large loud speakers in windows of the National building and as many as care to can assemble in front of the building and enjoy the broadcast.

These horns or speakers forming the Western Electric public address system reproduces the music perfectly and can be heard for more than a block away. Mr. C. S. Powell, sales manager of the W. E. Company in Nashville, is installing the system, and those who would like to hear WSM's inaugural program or part of it may do so through these loud speakers.

After opening night WSM extends a cordial invitation to everybody to visit the new studio during broadcasting hours or between. A comfortable auditorium has been prepared to take adequate care of a normal audience, and visitors will be heartily welcomed after October 5 at any time to listen to the concerts being given by Nashville artists through WSM.

WSM
Mammoth Dedication Program
7 P.M. to 2 A.M.

7:00 to 8:00 P. M.

1. Opening Announcement of Station—Mr. Edwin W. Craig, Vice-President of the National Life & Accident Insurance Co.
2. Prayer—Dr. O. E. Goddard, Pastor of the West End Methodist Church.
3. Shrine Band—Playing the National Anthem.
4. Dedicatory Message—President C. A. Craig of the National.
5. Music—The Shrine Band.
6. Brief Message—Gov. Austin Peay.
7. Song—Joseph Tant Mcberson, Concert Baritone, with Miss Hattie Paschal, Piano Accompanist.
8. Brief Message—Maj. D. B. Carson, Commissioner of Navigation, Washington, D. C.
9. Song—Joseph Tant McPherson, Baritone; Miss Paschal, Accompanist.
10. Brief Message—Mayor Hilary E. Howse of Nashville.
11. Song—Joseph Tant McPherson, Baritone; Miss Paschal, Accompanist.
12. Brief Message—Maj. Walter Van Nostrand, Supervisor of Radio Fourth District.
13. Instrumental Trio—Including Mrs. Horace Olson, Cello; Miss Alline Fentress, Violin; Miss Hattie Paschal, Piano.

8:00 to 8:30 P. M.

Famous Fisk Jubilee Quintet of Fisk University. Brief Message by Dr. A. F. Shaw, Dean.

8:30 to 9:00 P. M.

Beasley Smith's Andrew Jackson Orchestra.

9:00 to 10 P. M.

Knights of Columbus Vocal Quartet—Including Eugene Cunningham, First Tenor; John A. Dowd, Second Tenor; Eugene Murphy, Baritone; Vernon S. Arrington, Bass, and Bill Copeland, Piano Accompanist.

Instrumental Trio—Including Mrs. Horace Olson, Cellist; Miss Alline Fentress, Violinist, and Miss Hattie Paschal, Pianist.

Miss Aleda Waggoner, Soprano Soloist.

Vincent Kuhn, Vocalist.

10:00 to 11:00 P. M.

Mrs. Daisy Hoffman, Concert Pianist and Duo-Art Artist.

Mrs. Thomas J. Malone, Jr., Concert Soprano.

Mr. Kenneth Rose, Violin Soloist and Director of the Violin Department at Ward-Belmont.

Mrs. Kenneth Rose, Concert Pianist and Member of the Ward-Belmont Faculty.

Mrs. Robert Caldwell, Contralto Soloist of the West End Methodist Church Choir.

Mr. Milton Cook, Baritone Soloist of the First Presbyterian Church Choir.

11:00 P. M. to 12:00 M.

Francis Craig's Columbia Record Orchestra, with Vocal and Instrumental Soloists.

12:00 M. to 2 A. M.—Jamboree

Miss Bonnie Barnhardt, "The Lady of the Radio," Singer of Southern Melodies.

Jack Keefe, Popular Entertainer.

Joe Combs, Tenor Soloist.

Ted Stover, Syncopating Pianist.

W. J. Keshner, Saxophone Soloist.

Francis Craig's Columbia Recording Orchestra.

Other Features.

The National Life & Accident Insurance Company
(INCORPORATED)
NASHVILLE, TENNESSEE

had purchased most of the bend, about 1,400 acres. Before John Pennington, the McSpadden family had owned the bend, and before them, it was part of a land grant parceled out when Nashville was settled in 1779-80. In fact, just across the river from the bend, Fort Union had been constructed during Nashville's frontier days, and nearby, the first school and the first church located west of the Cumberland Mountains had been organized a few years after the fort's establishment.

Before the coming of the Anglo settlers, however, Pennington Bend, like most of Middle Tennessee, was home to a sizable prehistoric Indian population.

Born to Tradition

If Opryland Hotel seems a part of Americana at a relatively young age, credit its roots in the widely known and acclaimed Grand Ole Opry, in pioneer Nashville radio station WSM, and in a region's cherished reputation for gracious hospitality.

WSM was born in 1925 when Nashville-based National Life and Accident Insurance Company started experimenting with a new invention, radio, at the urging of Edwin W. Craig, son of company founder C.A. Craig. The company located the studio of one of the South's most powerful AM stations on the fifth floor of its corporate office building and hired the best announcer in the country, George D. Hay, to manage it.

Hay understood the need for programs to serve not only Nashville's culture-loving citizens but the large rural audience that also received the station's powerful signal. When white-bearded fiddler Uncle Jimmy Thompson played before WSM's microphones in late 1925, the foundation for the Grand Ole Opry was laid. The formal name came two years later as a parody of a grand opera broadcast.

WSM and the Opry grew in tandem. In 1932, WSM became a 50,000-watt station whose clear-channel signal covered much of the U.S. at night. The Opry roster of

Attracted by the fertile river-bottom soil, an abundance of streams flowing into the Cumberland River and the many species of game native to the region, these Indians, most likely of the Archaic and Woodland cultures, maintained several village and burial sites throughout the bend.

For many years after the McSpaddens, Pennington Bend was populated by only a few clans, among them the Pennington, Williamson, Nichols, and Graves families. By the turn of the 20th century, two other families who would become prominent in the region, the Rudys and the Strassers, had purchased large holdings in Pennington Bend. The Rudy family became known throughout the South for its commercial production of country-style sausage, while the Strassers concentrated on turning their farm into a quality dairy operation.

In the early 1960s, the Briley Parkway project was begun in Nashville to encircle the city with a four-lane highway. By the mid-1960s, the section planned through Pennington Bend to connect the neighborhoods of Donelson and Inglewood was nearly complete. The parkway bridge spanning the Cumberland River and replacing the Williamson Ferry had been dedicated.

entertainers, meanwhile, continued to grow. Roy Acuff joined the program in 1938, and a year later NBC radio decided to carry a half hour of the show on Saturday nights, bringing it to homes across the country.

The Opry left National Life's building when insurance company executives had difficulty entering their own offices in the crush of fans, eventually finding a home at Nashville's rambling, downtown Ryman Auditorium. From 1943 to 1974, Ryman audiences and WSM listeners heard country music legends Ernest Tubb and Eddy Arnold, Hank Williams and Bill Monroe, Porter Wagoner and George Jones, Loretta Lynn and Tammy Wynette. When the Opry occupied its new home

In the months following National Life's decision to build Opryland USA with WSM, Val Smith and others searched diligently for a parcel of land that met five criteria: the real estate had to be located fairly close to Nashville, preferably in Davidson County; the terrain had to be relatively flat and conducive to a large-scale construction project; the property must be large enough to support the three initial phases of the complex, plus future expansion; the site had to be easily accessible to the public, and it had to be close to a large body of water for aesthetic purposes and for a possible river way to downtown Nashville. To locate such property in the fastest growing region of Tennessee—an area dominated by rolling hills consisting mainly of limestone—proved a sizable challenge.

After several months of fruitless searching in areas around Nashville, Val Smith and a companion were aboard Smith's private plane one day when Smith decided to take a short detour over Pennington Bend. He noticed the unfinished highway construction that soon would be Briley Parkway, and his eyes fell on a vast expanse of flat farmland situated between the muddy roadbed and the Cumberland River, just south of the parkway's exit at McGavock Pike. Smith

that adjoins Opryland Hotel, Opry performers could be seen on television, not just heard on radio.

Tradition-rich WSM also found its way to the Opryland Hotel complex, locating the station's business and production headquarters at the corner of the hotel entrance and McGavock Pike. Nashville's most popular morning radio program, WSM's "The Waking Crew," was broadcast from the hotel's Stage Door Lounge, now Rusty's Sports Bar, until 1986. Popular performers were regular guests for the mix of live music and humorous conversation. In 1984, WSM-AM acquired studio space inside the hotel near the Magnolia Lobby entrance. Hidden from view behind the AM studio is country station WSM-FM.

Opryland Hotel is also rooted in the Nashville tradition of Southern hospitality. Combining touches of Old World elegance (the carpet in the Magnolia Lobby, for instance, was based on a traditional British pattern) and Deep South charm (from chandeliers to plantings), the hotel aims to delight and refresh its guests. Conveying that message is a staff steeped in the courteous and immaculate ways of the South. Among them are the "Tradition Makers" — employees on staff since the hotel first opened its doors in 1977, who bear the flame of gracious service that is the hotel's hallmark.

immediately realized that, if this parcel were available, it fit all five criteria—proximity (less than seven miles from downtown Nashville), water, flatness, size, and accessibility—to a "T."

Inquiry revealed most of the property Smith saw was available. The part facing McGavock Pike that extended from Briley Parkway to the river belonged to the former owner of the WSIX radio station in Nashville and housed an engineering building and three transmission towers. Within a matter of months and after considerable negotiation, National Life had purchased most of the land recommended

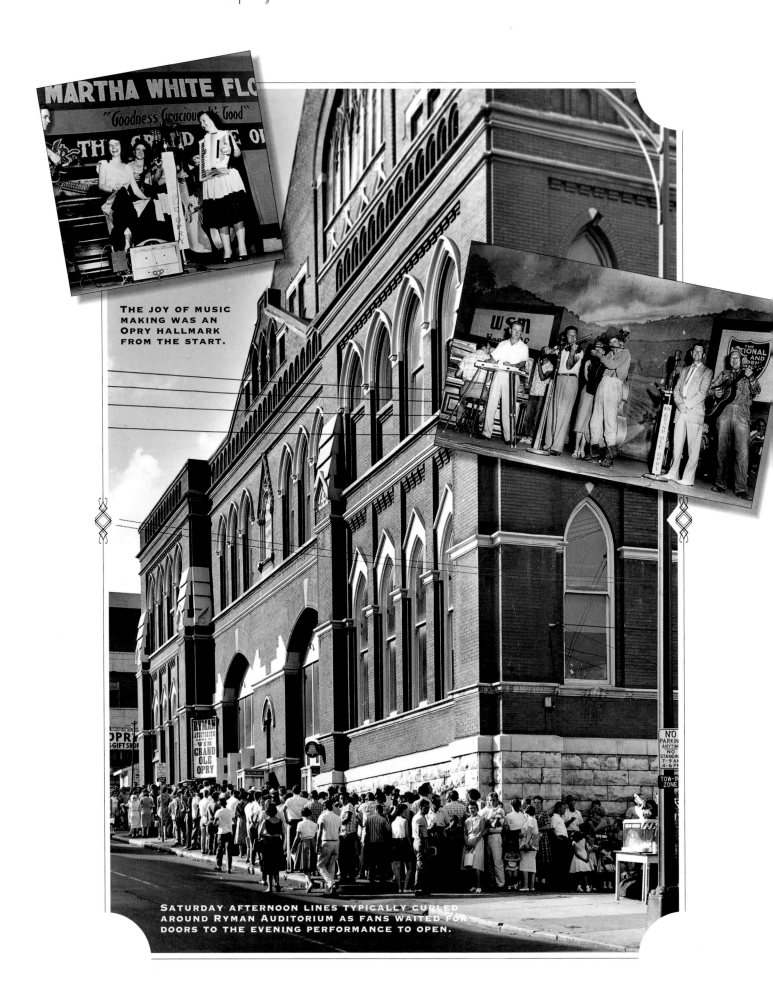

THE JOY OF MUSIC
MAKING WAS AN
OPRY HALLMARK
FROM THE START.

SATURDAY AFTERNOON LINES TYPICALLY CURLED
AROUND RYMAN AUDITORIUM AS FANS WAITED FOR
DOORS TO THE EVENING PERFORMANCE TO OPEN.

THE NEW OPRY HOUSE, WHICH OPENED IN 1974, WAS BUILT
ON THE INTERNATIONAL SUCCESS OF SUCH OPRY LEGENDS
AS PATSY CLINE AND HANK WILLIAMS.

by Smith, a chunk of real estate that would eventually total 425 acres.

National Life, WSM, and city officials broke ground for Opryland USA on

FROM LEFT, DAVE OVERTON, IRVING WAUGH, WILLIAM C. WEAVER JR., GOV. BUFORD ELLINGTON, G. DANIEL BROOKS AND MAYOR BEVERLY BRILEY PARTICIPATED IN THE 1970 OPRYLAND PARK GROUNDBREAKING.

June 30, 1970. Over the next year, attendance at the Grand Ole Opry's Ryman Auditorium on Fifth Avenue in downtown Nashville reached almost 400,000. The Ryman, built in 1891 as a tabernacle for visiting preachers, had been the home of the Opry since 1943 and was in a terrible state of repair. Uncomfortable "pew" seating, a leaking roof, substandard restrooms and no air conditioning were just a few of the structural deficiencies that required immediate attention if the Opry was to continue to call the building "home."

Accordingly, National Life officials decided that the second phase of Opryland USA's master plan, the construction of the new Opry house, should begin as soon as possible. On May 27, 1972, the park opened, drawing 10,000 visitors on the first day. Shortly afterward, construction on the Grand Ole Opry House was begun.

Several weeks before the end of Opryland USA's first season, when almost 1.5 million visitors had passed through the turnstiles, it was clear to National Life and

ANOTHER PACKED CROWD AT THE DOWNTOWN RYMAN AUDITORIUM

WSM management that attendance would far exceed projections. The question arose whether recommendations in the original feasibility report for the third phase—Oprytown and its associated motel—were still valid. In late 1972, Smith considered the report carefully and concluded that a new feasibility study, one that took into account the overwhelming success of the park's first season, was in order.

Based on revised facts and figures, the new feasibility study suggested that the size of the proposed hostelry, tentatively referred to as Oprytown Motel, be increased to accommodate from 400 to 600 rooms with the capability to expand to 1,000 units. It was further proposed that the parcel of Opryland USA real estate formed by the intersection of Briley Parkway and McGavock Pike (the site of present-day Opryland Hotel) be set aside for the development of Oprytown, the mini-village proposed as the third phase of the original study, and the adjoining motel.

1 9 7 5

AN EARLY SKETCH OF THE HOTEL'S FACADE BY ARCHITECT EARL SWENSSON

In fall 1975, work was launched to clear and prepare the McGavock Pike/Briley Parkway plot of land for construction. The project to be built was the Opryland Hotel, its name changed to better reflect the size and luxury of the proposed complex. The following spring, National Life officials issued a press release which described the scale of the project:

The facility will be comprised of six separate buildings. A three-story "core" building will contain the main lobby, restaurants, shops, a three-and-one-half story galleria covered with a skylight, a ballroom seating up to 2,200 persons with a permanent stage, what may be Nashville's first and largest show lounge, and a separate 30,000-square-foot exhibition hall. Five free-standing buildings, ranging from three to five stories in height and connected by enclosed hallways, will provide 601 guest rooms and 14 sitting rooms. The hotel complex has been designed so that it can ultimately be expanded to a total of 1,000 rooms.

Assuring the city's residents that the decision to construct the facility was "another tangible expression of our faith in the future of Nashville, and especially in our booming tourist industry," William C. Weaver, chairman of the board of directors of the newly formed NLT Corporation, the holding company of both National Life and WSM, declared that Opryland Hotel would be "one of, if not, THE largest self-contained convention facilities between Chicago and Miami Beach."

To design and direct so ambitious a project required a seasoned hotelier with vision. NLT found that person in Jack Vaughn, who had recently left the Westin chain after managing its acclaimed Century Plaza Hotel in Los Angeles. When a friend mentioned NLT's search for a general manager of the Opryland Hotel project and the possibility of Vaughn's applying for the job, he declared with mock alarm: "Where the devil is Nashville? I don't think so." But conversations with Irving Waugh and Opryland USA and Grand Ole Opry General Manager E. W. "Bud" Wendell convinced a skeptical Vaughn to tour the site.

Standing on former pasture land near the Cumberland River, Vaughn quickly saw the future hotel's primary potential — not as a place for Opryland Park's summer patrons to spend a night but as a nationally known, centrally located hotel and convention center where groups of all sizes would book blocks of rooms throughout the year. Spurred by this vision, he signed on as general manager in May 1975 and set about choosing a plantation theme to give the hotel a distinctive Southern charm and human scale. Years later, he would declare that fate was at work in the hotel's success. "It was the best time in the world to build a hotel, and I had some of the best people in the world to do it with," he said. But Waugh redirected the credit: "In Jack Vaughn," he said, "we struck gold."

With Bud Wendell's blessing, Vaughn proceeded to create a model for the industry. Given the rare opportunity as a general manager to help design a facility two years before it was to open, the man with a sharp eye for detail helped select

Even before the official announcement confirming the hotel's construction had been made, the hotel staff had sold 50,000 room nights, totaling almost $3 million in business.

everything: maids' uniforms to salt-and-pepper shakers, carpet patterns to cutlery. The meticulous Vaughn created easy-to-clean sconces and placed the hotel's giant chandeliers on a winch-and-pulley system so they could be easily lowered and polished late at night when guests were asleep.

Vaughn knew the first concern of convention and trade shows was ample exhibit space, so square footage on Opryland Hotel blueprints was doubled for this purpose, and state-of-the-art audio-visual capabilities were installed. Vaughn said the hotel was in the position "to bid for more than 80 percent of all the nation's meetings and conventions." Even before the official announcement had been made confirming National Life's go-ahead for the hotel's construction, Vaughn, his director of sales and marketing, Mike Dimond, and the hotel sales staff had sold 50,000 room nights (a measure of actual room use), totaling almost $3 million in business, to future conventions that ranged from Ducks Unlimited to the American Chemical Society.

National Life's $25 million commitment to the construction, furnishing, and equipping of the hotel was the largest ever made by the company in the Nashville area. To supervise the huge project, a building committee was appoint-

The House That Jack Built

The man who directed Opryland Hotel's emergence as the largest hotel and convention center under one roof in the world and burnished its reputation for sales and service learned his trade from the ground up: parking cars, cleaning bathrooms and carrying bags.

It was at the stately Hotel Benson in his native Portland, Oregon, that Jack Vaughn, a former Marine sergeant who had taken a correspondence course in hotel management, took the first step toward becoming, in the eyes of many of his peers, the greatest hotelier of his time.

Vaughn loved the venerable Benson, where he held 22 positions from night auditor to doorman, performing many of these duties on his own time. They included calls with the hotel's salesman in an old English cab. "Hotels were just evolving from a cottage business to an industry," Vaughn says. "I knew that sales and marketing — getting people into the hotel — would one day be the lifeblood of our business."

He carried that understanding to Chicago, where he successfully managed the Continental Plaza, and to Los Angeles, where he ran the 710-room Century Plaza, three blocks from the city limits of Beverly Hills. His legendary attention to detail was sharpened at the facility he main-

ed, chaired by John H. Tipton, Jr., executive vice president for investments of National Life.

Assisting Tipton were Irving Waugh, president of WSM; Bud Wendell, general manager of Opryland USA and the Grand Ole Opry; Julio Pierpaoli, manager of Opryland USA; Jack Vaughn, general manager of the hotel; Val Smith, by then the vice president and manager of National Life's real estate department; and Andrew T. Sutton, second vice president and manager of National Life's buildings division.

The architectural design for Opryland Hotel was awarded to two Nashville firms: Earl Swensson & Associates and Architect-Engineers Associates, headed by Charles Warterfield. Swensson was charged with designing the five guest buildings, all the guest rooms, and the exterior of the entire hotel complex. Warterfield tackled meeting rooms, exhibit areas, administrative offices, and the lobby. Construction of the hotel was awarded to two Nashville contractors: Hardaway Construction Company and Joe M. Rodgers

tained "to the gnat's eyebrow." Its marketing slogan: "The most beautiful hotel in the world."

What ultimately convinced Vaughn to trade the glamour of the West Coast for Nashville, where only hotel sketches and a cow-pasture site awaited, were the people who came calling on his services. E.W. "Bud" Wendell, Opryland USA general manager, traveled cross-country to meet Vaughn in the richly appointed lobby of the Beverly Hilton Hotel for an interview.

"'Boy, this is a fancy place,'" Vaughn recalls Wendell saying. "He was down to earth, with no airs about him," says Vaughn. "I knew I liked this guy." Vaughn spent a week in Nashville discussing the project with Opryland officials. "I just liked everything about them and the project," he says.

Jack Vaughn's enthusiasm was kindled. "I realized that three interstates intersected at Nashville, that it was within a day's drive of half the nation's population, and that there wasn't a true convention center in the state," he says. "I thought, 'Wow, if we could build a convention hotel here, something unique, with zing and pizzaz, we could knock their socks off.'"

And so they did.

& Associates. Hardaway was responsible for the Warterfield-designed aspects, while Rodgers spearheaded the Swensson-designed elements.

Earl Swensson and Charles Warterfield were acutely aware of the challenges they faced with the design of the Opryland Hotel. Swensson conceded that major convention hotels without immediate access to metropolitan areas were scarce in the country. "In the last two or three years there has been a move to the suburban-rural areas," he noted. "Yet there is the belief that exciting convention facilities exist only in downtown areas. What we are doing here is developing a completely

PHASE II, THE GLASS-
ROOFED CONSERVATORY,
RISES IN 1984

MCMLXXXIV

OPRYLANDHOTEL

TWO DECADES OF GROWTH
BEGAN WITH PHASE I, THE
ORIGINAL HOTEL, IN 1977

PHASE III, THE CASCADES, OPENS IN 1988

PHASE IV FEATURES THE MAMMOTH DELTA ADDITION, IN 1996

new concept in the convention and hotel industry."

Warterfield added that "between the two firms, we have fulfilled a rather demanding set of design assignments given us by the client." He revealed that the solution was not a high-rise structure but "a sprawling complex, an expansion of Opryland Park, with the convention-center complex blending into the overall Opryland landscape with its close alliance with nature and open spaces. Yet the entire facility is ultra-modern and functional."

1 7 9 7

There was a time when finding a good hotel room in Nashville was a difficult task. Francis Baily, an Englishman, who in later life became a founder of the Royal Astronomical Society of Great Britain, passed through the 17-year-old town in 1797 and wrote:

> There we met with good fare, but very poor accommodations for lodgings; three or four beds of the roughest construction in one room, which was open at all hours of the night for the reception of any rude rabble that had a mind to put up at the house; and if the other beds happened to be occupied, you might be surprised when you awoke in the morning to find a bedfellow by your side whom you had never seen before, and perhaps might never see again. All complaint is unnecessary…[and] your landlord may tell you that if you do not like it you are at liberty to depart as soon as you please.

Louis-Philippe, Duke of Orleans, was also a visitor to Nashville in 1797. His complaints were similar to Francis Baily's, as he declared:

> In Nashville we lodged at Captain Maxwell's. We would have been comfortable enough there if court had not been in session; as it was, the house was full, and even sleeping on the floor, there was hardly room.

Louis-Philippe never forgot his Nashville visit, and in later years, as king of France, he derived much good-natured pleasure by inquiring of American visitors to his court in Paris: "Do they still sleep three in a bed in Tennessee?"

By the time the Civil War engulfed Nashville, the town had grown into one of the most important inland communities in America. Fortunately for visitors, its lodging facilities had improved greatly since the early settlement days. The Maxwell House Hotel, at the corner of Fourth Avenue and Church Street, was begun in the days prior to the war, but its construction was delayed by the protracted conflict. In 1869 the luxurious hostelry opened for business with a menu featuring stuffed pig, lamb with mint sauce, and prairie grouse with currant jelly. It was the hotel's special blend of coffee served over the years that inspired Theodore Roosevelt to describe the delicious brew as "good to the last drop," a phrase that remains the slogan for Maxwell House coffee.

1 9 7 5

Official Nashville, as well as the local citizenry, was elated by National Life's decision to add a top-quality hotel to its already successful Opryland USA complex. The city, rapidly approaching a population of one-half million, had for years been called "The Athens of the South" for its abundance of colleges, universities and other cultural institutions. Likewise, in years past, it had been known for its quality downtown hotels. However, with America's flight to the suburbs, the advent of shopping malls and the positioning of motels and restaurants at practically every interstate exit, downtown Nashville, like most other large cities across the country, had suffered an erosion of its visitor base, both local and out-of-town. Consequently, few tourists or conventioneers availed themselves of the city's hotel facilities.

THE MAXWELL HOUSE HOTEL EMBELLISHED NASHVILLE'S REPUTATION FOR FINE ACCOMMODATIONS.

When the Opryland Hotel was announced, only one vintage hotel, the Hermitage, located at Sixth Avenue and Union Street, still operated in downtown Nashville. Other distinguished hostelries—the Andrew Jackson, Noel, Tulane, James Robertson, Sam Davis and the Maxwell House—had fallen by the wayside.

Built in 1910 in the classic Beaux Arts style, the Hermitage featured Italian sienna marble at its entrance, sand-colored brick outside and Russian walnut paneling inside. When built in 1910, it was located across Union Street from a beautifully landscaped park that connected the hotel with the impressive Tennessee State Capitol building, perched on a hill overlooking the city. In later years, the park had been replaced by Legislative Plaza, a partially underground building that houses offices for members of the state legislature and their staffs.

Francis Craig, an early bandmaster, hosted a live NBC radio show from the Hermitage for more than 15 years and went on to become internationally famous during the 1940s. Craig made the hotel his headquarters and provided nightly entertainment for private parties, dances and other social functions. During its heyday, the old hotel's corridors echoed with the voices of statesmen, presidents, gangsters and entertainment greats, among them, Franklin D. Roosevelt, Al Capone, Jack Dempsey and Bette Davis. Another celebrity, Winchester, Tennessee, native Dinah Shore, made her singing debut at the Hermitage Hotel with the Craig band in 1946.

1 9 7 7

The Opryland Hotel, soon to be a worthy successor to Nashville's long line of outstanding hostelries, greeted its first guests on November 26, 1977. By that time, the hotel had added key staff members, among them: Joe Henry, an experienced hotelier, as resident manager of the complex; Mike Dimond, as director of sales and marketing; and

Margaret Parker, former executive secretary to WSM President Irving Waugh, as corporate sales manager.

They were part of a talented and spirited team that would guide the hotel's meteoric rise. Dimond courted convention groups across America. "Mike put the hotel on the map," Vaughn would later say. He was helped by the irrepressible Parker, who helped create a bond between the hotel and the business community and brought a vivacious charm to hotel activities. Meanwhile, the ebullient Vaughn and his low-key, second-in-command, Henry, made the perfect odd couple. "I'd spin-wheel up to the ceiling," recalls Vaughn of his excitable nature, "and Joe would say, 'Are you finished now,' bringing me back to earth."

"Bud Wendell allowed us to be the success we are. All he had to do was say 'no' to our ideas, and they would have vanished. But he allowed us to dream and gave us the autonomy to succeed or fail."

—Jack Vaughn

Standing behind this energetic group was Bud Wendell. He had joined National Life in 1950 as an insurance agent posted in Ohio before moving to the Nashville home office to work for John H. DeWitt. He soon was placed in charge of the Ryman Auditorium and Opryland Park successively. In 1978, he succeeded Irving Waugh as president of the Opryland complex, which included the hotel. "Bud Wendell allowed us to be the success we are," Vaughn declares. "All he had to do was say 'no' to our ideas and they would have vanished. But he allowed us to dream, and gave us the autonomy to succeed or fail. Without Bud Wendell, this hotel would be maybe 1,000 rooms."

When the first guests arrived at the Opryland Hotel, they encountered

CHEF WEHRNER GLUR ARRANGES THE FARE FOR THE HOTEL'S OPENING BANQUET, IN 1977.

OPPOSITE PAGE: THE HOTEL'S CULINARY TALENT WAS HONORED BY THE PRESTIGIOUS EUROPEAN CHEF'S GUILD.

an impressive sight. The Williamsburg-inspired architecture of the hotel, whose entrance was situated along a circular driveway, gave guests the impression of a colonial governor's palace rather than a modern, state-of-the-art hotel. The interior of the Magnolia Lobby was equally imposing. Dominated by a grand staircase that descended from the mezzanine to the main floor from two directions before joining into a single flight of stairs halfway down, the spacious lobby and its magnificent chandelier would have done any European castle proud.

Four restaurants and bars—Rachel's Kitchen, the Old Hickory Restaurant, the Old Fashion Pickin' Parlor, and the Stage Door Lounge—were readily accessible from the lobby by following a wide corridor past several gift shops and boutiques, all beneath a three-story atrium with a large skylight. The Old Hickory Restaurant, particularly, was heralded by Nashville's press as an outstanding addition to the area's fine eating establishments. "A meal in the Old Hickory Restaurant," declared one reporter, "reminds one of the genteel dining customs of the Old South." Another declared its "rose and striped wallpaper with matching upholstery on the Queen Anne furniture and the table appointments bring to mind the elegance of 1829 when Andrew Jackson assumed the presidency."

Continuing down the corridor past the Old Hickory Restaurant, guests arrived at the Tennessee Ballroom, consisting of 20,000 square feet of meeting space. Gracing the walls of the ballroom's lobby was a series of ceiling-to-floor murals depicting Nashville in the 1890s and painted by Max Hochstetler, an associate art professor at Austin Peay State University in nearby Clarksville. Beneath the ballroom, on the basement level, was a 30,000-square-foot exhibit area. Outside, adorning the manicured lawn, was a variety of native trees and shrubs. Four tennis courts and a swimming pool were easily accessible to guests seeking recreational activities.

Guests would have been impressed by the Opryland Hotel's physical statistics: buildings that covered 12.5 acres, contained 1.5 million exterior bricks and 113 miles of wiring. But just as impressive as the scale of the hotel were its elegant touches. The pattern of the carpet in the Magnolia Lobby dated to the 17th century and was made for the hotel by

JURIED WORKS BY TENNESSEE
ARTISTS PORTRAYING HOME-STATE
THEMES ARE PERMANENTLY
DISPLAYED THROUGHOUT THE HOTEL.

"ERNEST TUBB" BY VAN CORDLE

"NASHVILLE PAPER STOCK CO." BY
JONATHON DEFREES

"THE HAYRAKE" BY PAUL BROWN

"OLD GRIST MILL" BY MARJORIE SCHWARTZ

"A SONGWRITER'S PRAYER" BY KATA KOLLER

"TULIP FIELD"
BY ANDREW
MOORE

25

a British company that bore the seal of the royal family. The railings of the grand staircase were hand-turned, and the sconces in the corridors were custom-made. There were unique candelabras in the lobby, an English leaded-glass window as a shopfront, artful French posters on the walls, and locally hand-crafted breakfronts in the hallway.

Shortly after the grand opening, the hotel held an art competition among Tennessee artists with the goal of purchasing the best offerings to hang permanently throughout the facility. Fifty-three pieces were purchased for $50,000, forming the basis for the Opryland Hotel "Tennessee Art Collection." In 1991, 63 new pieces of artwork were acquired for $100,000 and displayed alongside the earlier examples of Tennessee-inspired art created by Tennesseans. In 1997, a third competition brought to 175 the number of artworks in the Opryland Hotel permanent collection.

1 9 7 9

In the hotel's first year of operation, 350,000 guests came through the doors. The average daily occupancy rate was 79.5 percent, compared to a national average among resort hotels of just over 70 percent. By the end of the first 12 months, hotel sales managers had booked 550,000 room nights, through 1985. In the hotel's second full year, 1979, the occupancy rate leaped to 86 percent. In January 1980, anticipating a major expansion, National Life officials purchased the 57 remaining acres between the hotel, McGavock Pike, and the Cumberland River, bringing to 425 the total acreage in the Opryland USA complex.

In April 1980, the Mobil Corporation bestowed its coveted "Four Star" status on Opryland Hotel, one of only five facilities in Tennessee so honored. The heavy tourist months of June, July and August brought with them a 98.9 percent occupancy rate, a record Jack Vaughn found "almost unbelievable." In September, prompted by the success of the hotel, National Life officials confirmed that expansion plans were under serious study.

On April 14, 1981, National Life made the long-awaited announcement: the Opryland Hotel would be enlarged by 419 guest rooms and 225,000 square feet of meeting and exhibition space, including a 77,000-square-foot exhibit hall and a 30,000-square-foot ballroom. Banquet facilities would be augmented to serve as many as 5,200 at a sitting, more than twice the previous capacity. The expanded hotel would accommodate 90 percent of all national conventions held in the United States. An impressive feature of the expansion plans was

THE HOTEL HARMONIOUSLY COM-BINED HOME-STYLE CORDIALITY AND ELEGANT TOUCHES, FROM UNUSUAL POSTER REPRODUCTIONS TO ORNATE FURNISHINGS.

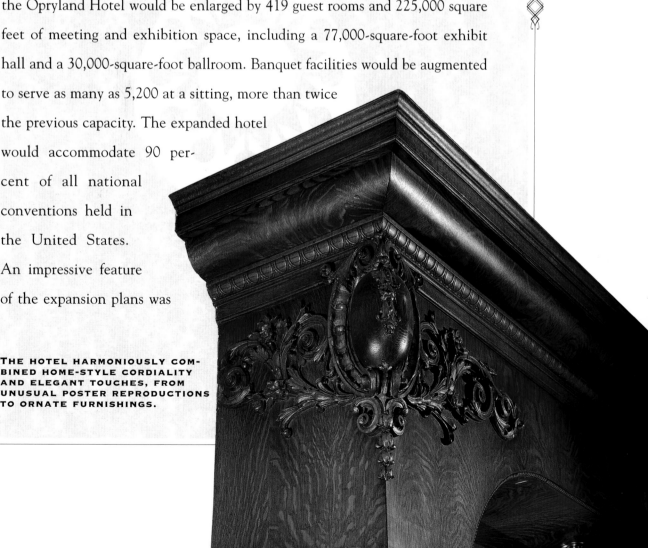

a seven-story atrium called the Conservatory, which would cover in glass a sub-tropical garden with a stream and a five-story fountain.

Charles Warterfield and Earl Swensson, architects for Phase I, were selected to design Phase II. Hardaway Construction, one of the Phase I general contractors, and another Nashville builder, Sharondale Construction, were chosen for the project. Target date for completion of Phase II was early 1984, at a price of $40 million.

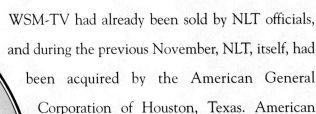

1 9 8 3

In early July 1983, while workmen put finishing touches to the huge glass roof that covered the 1.5-acre Conservatory, announcement was made in Nashville that confirmed what locals had suspected for some time. Edward L. Gaylord, an Oklahoma City businessman whose sizable holdings included radio and TV stations and daily newspapers across the country as well as television's "Hee Haw" show, had purchased the Opryland complex for a reported $240 million.

WSM-TV had already been sold by NLT officials, and during the previous November, NLT, itself, had been acquired by the American General Corporation of Houston, Texas. American General had no interest in owning and maintaining entertainment properties, preferring to concentrate on its primary business: insurance. Ed Gaylord made it clear from the beginning he intended to keep Bud Wendell at the helm of his new acquisition and had no plans for dramatic change in Opryland's management. He purchased a full-page ad in the *Wall*

EDWARD GAYLORD

Street Journal that declared: "On the day the papers were signed, an elegant lady from Grinder's Switch, Tenn., Miss Minnie Pearl, very wisely told us, 'If it ain't broke, don't fix it.' It ain't, so we won't. It doesn't need fixing."

The Gaylord conglomerate's conservative Southwestern heritage fit comfortably with Opryland's heartland values. Ed Gaylord's father, E. K., had purchased the *Daily Oklahoman* in Oklahoma City in 1903 when the state was still a frontier territory. From this newspaper and its Oklahoma Publishing Company sprang an empire. The company acquired radio and television stations in major markets and further diversified by adding real estate and oil and gas divisions. In the 1970s, Gaylord

Phase III would add almost 800 guest rooms, create 300 additional jobs and cost $30 million. Total room count when Phase III was complete would be 1,891, making the Opryland Hotel one of the largest hostelries in the country.

Production Company was established in Los Angeles to supply the television stations with quality programs. Opryland became a crown jewel in the Gaylord holdings, enhancing its presence in the hospitality and entertainment industries.

No sooner had the doors to Opryland Hotel's Phase II formally opened in early 1983 than Bud Wendell announced that his management team was seriously considering a Phase III building project. Phase II brought the total number of guest rooms to 1,064, along with 37 additional meeting rooms and a new, 18,500-square-foot pre-function area. According to Wendell's announcement, Phase III would add almost 800 guest rooms, create 300 additional jobs and cost $30 million. Phase III would bring the room count to 1,891, making the Opryland Hotel one of the largest hostelries in the country.

Meanwhile, the new Conservatory was the talk of Nashville and the hundreds of out-of-town guests who lodged at the hotel daily. The glass-roofed tropical paradise contained 8,000 plants representing more than 200 species. Kept at a constant 71 degrees, the luxurious garden included streams, four waterfalls, and benches for strollers as they made their way along its paths. An officer of Sharondale Construction Company, the builder, predicted the Conservatory "will be one of the hotel's highlights," adding, "The design team for the hotel researched

The Man With the Plans

It was almost as a lark that Nashville architect Earl Swensson, known in the early 1970s for the stark modernism of his designs, created a colonial-Philadelphia look, with brick facade, dormers and a Liberty Bell theme, in a design competition for the Opryland Hotel.

"I had a ball doing it, but I knew it would never win," recalls Swensson, who had not designed a hotel before. To his surprise, the warm quality of his Philadelphia sketch caught the eye of Jack Vaughn, who was newly hired in the summer of 1975 as general manager of the yet-to-be-built Opryland Hotel. Vaughn felt, however, the Philadelphia motif didn't suit Nashville.

"What is Nashville known for?" Vaughn, a newcomer just-arrived from the West Coast, asked Swensson, who had moved to Nashville from Chicago 15 years earlier. "Isn't this plantation country? Why don't we come up with a plantation theme?

19th century European conservatories at length" before drawing final plans for Opryland's classic example.

For visitors whose ramblings in the rain forest-like atmosphere of the Conservatory had whetted an appetite, the new Phase II restaurant, Rhett's, along with the neighboring Jack Daniel's Saloon, were close by for food and drink. Rhett's projected a "Gone With the Wind" theme and featured such delicacies as "Ashley Wilkes Shrimp," "Gone With the Tail Wind Lobster," "Aunt Pitty Pat's Platter" and "James K. Polk Chops."

In December 1984, trying to bolster the Opryland Hotel's holiday-season appeal among visitors as well as home folks, officials initiated a program that has become a cherished Nashville tradition. "A Country Christmas" first opened to the public December 7th and ran for 17 days. The extravaganza featured a traditional arts, crafts and antiques show; holiday storytelling sessions with Grand Ole Opry stars; a major Christmas musical production; and construction of a miniature Christmas village. Local choirs sang Christmas carols in the Conservatory, which was described as "a sea of poinsettias." At the entrance to the hotel, thousands of lights decorated a 50-foot-tall blue spruce Christmas tree

On successive days, Swensson showed Vaughn two views of the South. They flew to Savannah, with its riverside docks and rural south Georgia flavor, then visited Williamsburg, Virginia, for a look at its formal, colonial-era buildings. Along the way, they talked and Swensson sketched, combining the romantic elements of Williamsburg and the intimacy of Savannah.

The result of the trip was 13 sketches which Swensson laid out on a floor and Vaughn rejected, one after another, until he suddenly stood before what would materialize two years later as

donated by the citizens of New Brunswick, Canada. The whole idea of "A Country Christmas," according to Jack Vaughn, was to "make the Opryland Hotel a major holiday destination."

On October 22, 1985, Opryland officials formally announced the major Phase III expansion of the hotel. It would add 700 guest rooms (later expanded to 824), six meeting rooms, 40,000 square feet of exhibit space, a ballroom, 12 shops and a spectacular waterscape called the Cascades. Construction would begin in early 1986 with completion in 1988, at a projected cost of $55 million.

About this time, Opryland unveiled a floating venue that immediately became a signature attraction: the sternwheeler, General Jackson. Built for Opryland by Jeffboat in Jeffersonville, Indiana, the elegant, triple-deck showboat could cruise the Cumberland with 1,200 guests and crew aboard. Conventioneers and other guests were treated to live entertainment and sit-down dinners in a setting that captured the flavor of the Mark Twain-era of river life. In the pilot house stood the boat's first captain, whose name really was Edgar Allan Poe.

Capitalizing on the immense popularity of "A Country Christmas," officials made plans in mid-1985 to again offer the holiday festivity. The hotel enjoyed an

the distinctive look of the Opryland Hotel. "That's it!" Vaughn cried out. "I've never seen anything like it, but it feels right."

This intuitive method would be repeated when the idea for creating the first of the hotel's huge garden atriums, the Conservatory, was broached. Swensson had each member of the evaluation team name a favorite glass-roofed environment that the group could visit. Besides American hotels, mansions and gardens, the list included sites in Acapulco, London and Milan.

From the trips and comments, Swensson formulated his design. His goal was to create a "springtime in the park" ambience. There would be huge plants and a walkway in the air. Hotel rooms would provide the garden's backdrop, and each room would have a balcony looking inward — a revolutionary idea for the time.

As daring as were the scale and features of the garden, it, too, became a reality. "We had established a pattern," said Swensson, adding: "I would never have conceived it if Jack hadn't said: 'I've got to have that!', and Bud Wendell hadn't become convinced it would work!"

87 percent occupancy rate for the year and ranked among the top ten convention centers in the nation, according to readers of *Corporate Meetings and Incentives* magazine. Those accomplishments, together with the gala Christmas affair, helped close the Opryland Hotel's 1985 season on a high note.

1 9 8 7

By mid-1987, Phase III of the Opryland Hotel's master plan was well under way. Its most talked-about feature was the Cascades, a six-story atrium covered by an acre of glass — some 3,000 panes, each measuring three-and-a-half by five feet. Originally planned to cover one-half acre, the indoor garden had been expanded to two acres. Installation of the glass posed several challenges, including how best to lift heavy crates con-

taining the panes high into the air and onto the roof of the atrium. When it came time to put the glass in place, the contractors hired a helicopter service whose pilot carefully hauled each heavy crate of glass from the ground to the top of the building.

THE LAUNCH OF THE HOTEL'S ORNATE STERNWHEELER FROM AN INDIANA SHIPYARD.

Each round-trip took two minutes, and the time involved to lift all the glass onto the roof was far less than using conventional cranes. By the end of the 20th day, after the helicopter had hoisted the last of the glass to the top, 25 highly-skilled glaziers had installed all 3,000 panes in the 328- by 165-foot skylight — without the loss of a single pane.

The rest of the hotel's construction was on schedule as well. As November 1987, the Opryland Hotel's 10th birthday, approached, the facility was on its way to becoming the 12th largest hotel in the United States. To commemorate the first decade of operation, Opryland management announced that the cost for the all-you-can-eat Sunday Brunch for November 29 would be rolled back to 1977 prices: $5.95 for adults and $3.95 for children. Before the day was over, nearly 5,000 patrons had

THE GENERAL JACKSON BECAME AN OPRYLAND ICON.

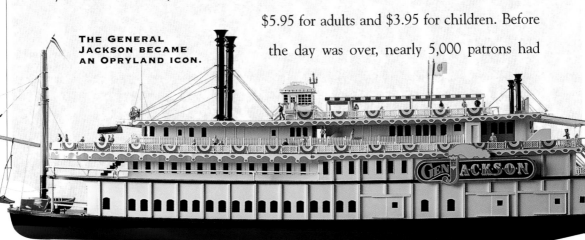

partaken of the fare, some of them waiting in line for two hours for the feast served in lavish Southern style in the hotel's main corridor.

In spring 1988, the Opryland Hotel was named one of the nation's "Ten Best Conference Centers." Professionalism of the staff, quality of equipment and originality of design were factors considered by 40,000 readers of *Corporate Meetings and Incentives* magazine, who voted in the competition. Other award winners were such prestigious properties as the Colonial Williamsburg Hotel in Williamsburg, Virginia; the Four Seasons Hotel and Resort in Dallas; the Broadmoor Hotel in Colorado Springs; and the Greenbrier in White Sulphur Springs, Virginia. The

In August 1988, Gaylord Entertainment announced that Larry Nelson, a U.S. Open and two-time PGA champion, had been chosen to design the course to be called the Springhouse Golf Club.

year 1988 also marked the tenth consecutive year that Opryland was selected one of the top ten convention hotels in the U.S.

As expected, when Phase III construction was complete in early spring of 1988 and the hotel opened the doors to its new wing, the sight was breathtaking. The glass-domed Cascades was surrounded by 824 new rooms overlooking the lush tropical gardens, waterfalls and 12,500-square-foot lake. A restaurant, a lounge housed in a revolving gazebo, a spectacular light and music show, and expanded meeting and exhibit space rounded out the $55 million addition.

1 9 8 8

Despite Opryland Hotel's high annual occupancy rate and a multitude of hotel and convention center awards, hotel officials bemoaned the absence of a world-class golf course. The Greenbrier, the Williamsburg Inn, the Broadmoor and other outstanding American resorts maintained such courses as an additional attraction for tourists and conventioneers. However, the tract of land supporting the Opryland complex and several administrative buildings was rapidly filling up. Plans for additional hotel projects, other than expansion of the hotel itself, were limited by space.

SPRINGHOUSE GOLF CLUB DESIGNER LARRY NELSON (SECOND FROM RIGHT) INSPECTS PLANS FOR THE 18-HOLE COURSE.

To remedy the situation, negotiations began with a nearby landowner in early 1988 to purchase 220 acres in Pennington Bend a short distance from the hotel on the east side of Briley Parkway. As early as February, officials confirmed that the hotel had begun planning an 18-hole golf course and a clubhouse. In August 1988, Gaylord Entertainment announced that Larry Nelson, a U.S. Open and two-time PGA champion, had been chosen to design the course to be called the Springhouse Golf Club.

Mural, Mural on the Wall

An abstract artist with no experience as a muralist received the commission to produce the centerpiece of Opryland Hotel artworks: a series of realistic murals. By the end of the two-and-a-half-year project, T. Max Hochstetler had proved his mastery of the genre.

The murals, celebrating the Golden Era of Nashville architecture, cover 2,200 square feet of wall space and stand as a hotel attraction in themselves. Hotel walls also display 175 art pieces acquired during three competitions of Tennessee artists. Pen-and-ink drawings of Grand Ole Opry stars, done by Nashville architect John Black, form still another gallery in the hotel.

Hochstetler, who retired as professor of painting from Austin Peay State University in Clarksville, Tennessee in 1999, was invited to do the murals in 1976. Austin Peay not only granted him a sabbatical but also provided studio space on campus for the project which took 15 months of work spread over a 30-month period.

Seven students assisted Hochstetler on the murals, done in sections, like strips of wallpaper. "We worked on heavy cotton-duck canvas, 10-feet wide," says Hochstetler. "In all, we used over 200 yards of canvas."

"I'd like to make this course fun for people who don't play golf much, but I also want it to be fitting to hold a future PGA championship," declared Nelson at a local news conference, adding: "My goal is a course that will be highly enjoyable, both in terms of playability and aesthetics, for the resort golfer, and one that will be challenging to Tour players, too." The projected completion date was summer 1990. Mason Rudolph, a 21-year veteran of the PGA Tour, was named director of instruction.

On the day following the announcement of Springhouse Golf Club, Opryland management learned that readers of *Medical Meetings* magazine had selected the hotel as one of 40 facilities worldwide to receive the magazine's first annual "Merit and Distinction" award. In the company of the Broadmoor, the Acapulco Princess Hotel, the Breakers Hotel in Palm Beach, Florida, and Loew's Anatole Hotel in Dallas, Opryland was praised for the quality of its food, beverage and catering service, guest and meeting rooms, and audio-visual support. In making the announcement, Dean Laux, president and publisher of *Medical Meetings*, said the selection was "a tribute to the high regard the property has earned among our readers."

Charged with creating an historical work, Hochstetler selected Nashville architecture from the 1880s and 1890s as the subject for the murals, which decorate the walls of the Nashville Lobby, a reception area located outside the Tennessee Ballroom, site of many special events.

Nashville's old public square, Downtown Presbyterian Church, Belmont Mansion, Jubilee Hall at Fisk University and Union Station are among landmarks featured in the mural. To enliven his canvas, Hochstetler invented scenes on the buildings' grounds and populated them with people he knew. He took Polaroid shots of his family, colleagues — "whoever was handy and could pose," he says. From sketches based on the Polaroids, he painted activities surrounding the landmarks.

Hochstetler himself is in one of the panels — appropriately, as a sign painter, plying his trade on a ladder by the Woodland Street Bridge.

In September 1990, the Springhouse Golf Club held its grand opening. Boasting a 43,000-square-foot clubhouse in the style of a Southern plantation, the club opened its 18 holes of manicured fairways to guests at the Opryland Hotel the following week. As expected, the addition of a world-class golf course to its growing list of attractions and amenities made the hotel even more popular among conventioneers and tourists.

The 1990 year closed at the hotel with a greatly enhanced "A Country Christmas." The seventh annual celebration was expanded from 17 to 35 days, with

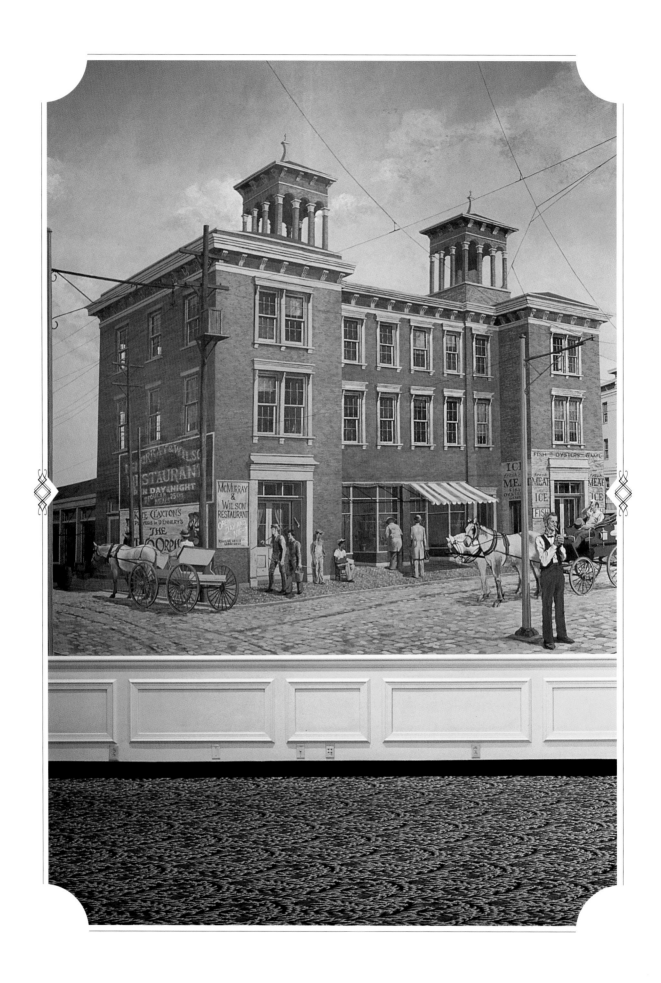

ARTIST T. MAX HOCHSTETLER'S MURAL OF
1890S-ERA NASHVILLE COVERS THE WALLS
OF THE HOTEL'S LARGE NASHVILLE LOBBY.

the festive event beginning the day before Thanksgiving. From modest beginnings, it had grown in many ways. Now, almost 1.5 million lights adorned trees both inside the hotel and out, and 3.2 miles of red ribbon and 4.5 miles of evergreen garland stretched across the hotel property, transforming the complex into a wonderland. The holiday menu in the Old Hickory Restaurant featured the specialty of a different country each night, adding Old World charm to the festivities.

When "A Country Christmas" 1990 ended, more than 500 groups and 200,000 people had enjoyed the hotel's holiday decor and the outstanding laser and music show presented in the glass-domed Cascades. If the first year of the decade was an indication, the Opryland Hotel's future was bright, indeed.

1 9 9 1

The year 1991 was a busy one for officials and staff at the hotel. A mini-expansion, adding nearly 39,000 square feet of meeting and office space at a cost of $3.1 million, was completed. In June, during a conference at the hotel of more than 700 advertising and marketing executives, President George Bush used satellite technology to address the gathering from the White House. "I wish I were there at Opryland," the President exclaimed, citing his love of country music and his close association with many of Nashville's performers. Also in June, Opryland Park's forty-millionth visitor, the Bill King family from Coppell, Texas, walked through the gates, and as a prize, received a free return trip to Nashville and lodging at the Opryland Hotel.

Even before its first anniversary, the Springhouse Golf Club was receiving rave reviews from business journals and travelers. The Opryland Hotel was honored in mid-summer 1991 as one of the nation's top 75 meeting destinations that offered golf. In making the recognition, *Meetings & Conventions* magazine cited the golf course's "difficulty, aesthetics, overall condition, carts, capabilities of the golf shop staff, quality of rental equipment, and ability of the golf staff to organize tournaments."

Meanwhile, the hotel's energetic sales staff had booked a variety of future conventions totaling an unprecedented two-million room nights. They included the National Association of Postmasters, with nearly 10,000 room nights; IBM, with 5,724 room nights; the American Correctional Association, with 15,525 room-nights; and the National Association of Realtors, with 9,558 room nights.

In September 1991, officials of Gaylord Entertainment, the parent company of the Opryland Hotel, announced the company would go public with an offering of nine million shares of stock valued at approximately $200 million. All nine million shares were sold on the first day of trading, as the price per share climbed from $20.50 to $23.13.

On October 7, 1991, President Bush fulfilled his wish to be at Opryland when he flew into Nashville for the nationally televised Country Music Association awards. The President was escorted from the airport to the Opryland Hotel, where he freshened up and changed into his tuxedo. He and Mrs. Bush reveled in country music's premier awards event, after which they rushed back to the airport to board Air Force One for the return trip to Washington, D.C.

1 9 9 2

In the fall of 1992, Jack Vaughn proudly announced that the Opryland Hotel had received yet another but totally different honor. *Successful Meetings* magazine had selected the hotel for its first ever Hospitality Industry Humanitarian Award. Vaughn, in accepting the tribute, called it "one of the most meaningful awards the hotel has ever received because it recognizes employees who voluntarily have gone beyond the call of duty to help others."

Selected from 29 North American hotels, resorts and convention centers, Opryland was cited for its variety of employee community projects, among them: horticultural employees' assisting local schools in landscaping their campuses, hotel restaurant employees' collecting and distributing food for needy families, and convention services employees' bringing Christmas presents to the homeless. "Nashville is certainly a better place to live because of their efforts," Vaughn declared.

At the time Vaughn was accepting the Humanitarian Award, remarkable statistics about the Opryland Hotel's first 15 years of operation were released. Since its opening, 9.3 million guests had stayed overnight, while more than 25 million people had walked its halls. Based on number of guest rooms, the Opryland Hotel was America's 12th largest. It boasted the largest exhibit facility inside a hotel in all of North America. And, finally, from the community perspective, since the hotel had opened in 1977, the number of convention-goers visiting Nashville had soared.

Though hints of another major expansion for the hotel had been in the air for a year, it wasn't until May 1993 that Phase IV was announced. Requiring an investment of nearly $200 million dollars, the construction would be the largest single project in Nashville's history, doubling the price tag of the towering BellSouth headquarters being built downtown. Citing "a tremendous demand for our type facility" and noting that the Opryland Hotel had turned away 450,000 guests over the past four years for lack of space, Jack Vaughn announced that Phase IV would add 979 guest rooms, bringing the total number to 2,884. Exhibit space would grow to 300,000 square feet, while 1,300 jobs would be created with

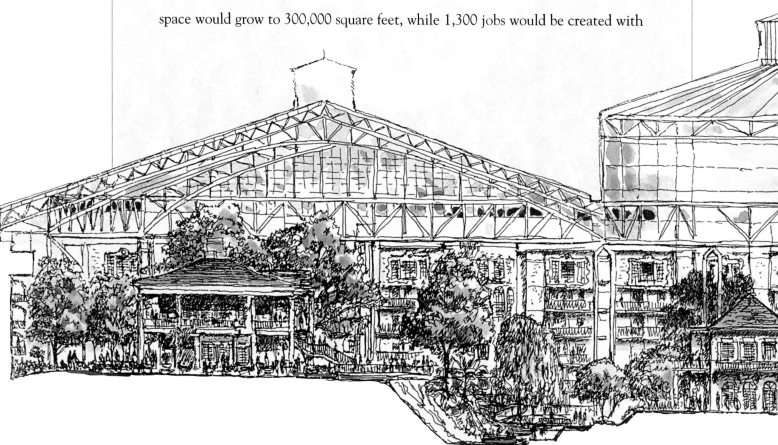

an additional payroll of almost $25 million.

As with Phases II and III, the news that delighted Nashvillians and former guests most was the creation of a new, glass-covered arboretum, similar to, but much larger than, the Conservatory and Cascades. Covering 4.5 acres, the new Delta would include an indoor river and lake system, an amphitheater, waterfalls, restaurants and a village of shops reminiscent of early New Orleans. Phase IV's announcement coincided with the annual meeting of Gaylord Entertainment shareholders. At that meeting, Gaylord Entertainment President Bud Wendell told listeners that, "While the hotel's Conservatory and Cascades are spectacular, to paraphrase Al Jolson, 'You ain't seen nothin' yet.'"

Earl Swensson, the Nashville architect involved in all of the hotel's previous design work, was selected to implement Phase IV as well. Reminiscing about the hotel's explosive growth, Swensson revealed that in the early days of operation, he thought the maximum number of rooms the facility could ever justify would be 1,000. Now, with three times that many on the horizon, he declared, "I hope we're going to be ahead of the pack by at least 10 years, and what happens after that, we'll have to just wait and see. But we'll be ready."

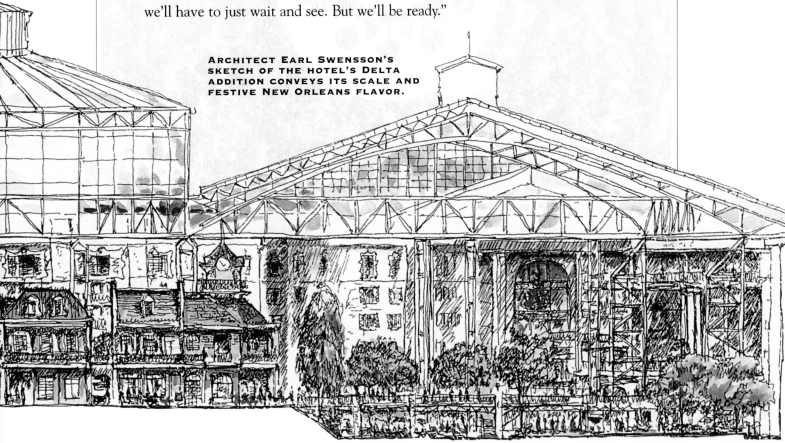

ARCHITECT EARL SWENSSON'S SKETCH OF THE HOTEL'S DELTA ADDITION CONVEYS ITS SCALE AND FESTIVE NEW ORLEANS FLAVOR.

1 9 9 4

During the summer of 1994, while Phase IV work was under way at the Opryland complex at Pennington Bend, Gaylord Entertainment introduced a feature that linked the hotel to downtown Nashville. For the past couple of years, Gaylord Entertainment, under Bud Wendell's leadership, had poured several million dollars into downtown Nashville, most of the money used to completely restore the Ryman Auditorium, home of the Grand Ole Opry for 31 years before it was moved to Opryland USA. Gaylord Entertainment had also purchased a site on historic Second Avenue, razed the existing building and built the Wildhorse Saloon, a combination country dance hall and nightclub. Said the *Nashville Tennessean* in tribute: "In a sense, Wendell helped put the music back in Music City."

THE WILDHORSE PUT A KICK INTO NASHVILLE'S URBAN REVIVAL.

Sometime earlier, other Nashville visionaries realized the important potential a restoration of the city's riverfront could have for growth of the tourist trade. Once the heart of Nashville's thriving business district, the area had suffered from years of neglect. But during the late 1980s and early 1990s, the decaying, Victorian-styled warehouses that lined First and Second avenues between Broad and Church

THE HOTEL'S SENIOR MANAGEMENT TEAM IN THE LATE 1980S INCLUDED, SEATED: JACK VAUGHN (LEFT) AND GEORGE AGUEL, AND STANDING, FROM LEFT: JOE HENRY, RICK STANFIELD, RUDY CADUFF, RAY WATERS AND MANFRED MORITZ.

streets were refurbished in a massive cleanup campaign that converted the virtually deserted district into a vibrant tourist destination of fine restaurants and shops. With the opening of the restored Ryman and the dedication of the new Wildhorse Saloon, Gaylord Entertainment Company had made a major commitment to the revival of Nashville's downtown area.

But downtown Nashville and the Opryland Hotel are seven miles apart, and Gaylord Entertainment planners debated ways of getting hotel guests to the Ryman, the Wildhorse and other downtown attractions and back again. A novel method of transportation, and the ultimate choice, consisted of two river taxis, each costing $750,000 and capable of carrying 149 passengers. Terminals for the water shuttle were built on the Cumberland River at Opryland and at Riverfront Park at the foot of Broad Street in downtown Nashville. Cruising quietly up and down the Cumberland, the taxis made the trip between terminals in 45 minutes.

In late October 1995, almost eight months ahead of schedule for the completion of the Opryland Hotel's Phase IV addition, 400 of the project's new guest rooms were opened to the public. In the meantime, it was announced that "A Country Christmas" had been expanded to run almost two full months, from November 1 to December 26, and would include activity at the Opryland Park. Besides featuring the world's largest Nativity scene, consisting of 75 larger-than-life figures, the event would include performances of Appalachian

How Does Your Garden Grow

The nine acres of gardens beneath Opryland Hotel's three glass-domed atriums boast 50,000 plants representing 445 species. Towering banana trees, patches of vibrant Amazon lilies, rows of pastel impatiens and perfumed gardenia, with nary a brown or droopy leaf among them, create a landscape that's an Opryland trademark.

This indoor paradise, including one of the best collections of tropical palms in the U.S., pays tribute to the labors of the horticultural staff and the foresight of the hotel founders.

"At the time the first garden, the Conservatory, was built, it was a new idea," says veteran Opryland horticulturist Hollis Malone. "There were small atriums in hotels, but this was quite daring: a $50 million investment to put glass over the two acres of gardens. But the architect, Earl Swensson, was confident people would be drawn to this kind of park, where you never had bad weather. He kept saying, 'It will work. It will work.'"

Indeed it has, time and again. The two-acre Conservatory

folk music, campfire storytelling, special concerts by Crystal Gayle and Eddie Rabbitt, an arts and crafts display, seasonal food at the restaurants and the daily presentation of "A Christmas Carol" at the nearby Acuff Theater.

By 1995, eleven years after "A Country Christmas" was first organized at the hotel, the event had become an annual must-see event for thousands of visitors who returned year after year to participate in the activities. The number of lights that graced the evergreens around the hotel had grown to 1.8 million, and the total length of the garland that draped every nook and cranny of the interior measured nine miles. Thirty thousand potted poinsettias festively adorned the Conservatory and Cascades.

As 1996 began, attention at the Opryland Hotel turned to the summer opening of the Delta. Hundreds of workers reported to the construction site seven days a week, as they had for more than two years, feverishly working to finish the project on time. Coordinated closely with the Delta's unveiling was the scheduling of one of the largest conventions ever hosted by the hotel, the 7,000-member Society of Television Cable Engineers, due to arrive on June 7.

One of the last elements to be completed was the planting of the many varieties of trees and flowers that adorn the Delta. With a budget of $1.7 million,

opened in 1983 with 8,000 plants and four water-falls. In 1988, the Cascades added another two acres of green, dominated by a 46-foot-tall mountain and a 12,500-square-foot lake.

The Delta, the largest garden, was completed in 1996. Seventy black olive trees, two mahogany trees, 170 sabal palm trees, three banana trees and over 500 lady palms thrive in the 4.5-acre Delta that includes a quarter-mile-long river flowing around an island at the bayou's center.

Opryland Hotel's director of horticulture, Hollis Malone, and his staff of gardeners oversaw the selection and successful planting of scores of different species, including 370 full-grown trees, some of them 20 to 40 years old and measuring up to 40 feet tall. The task of transporting this "Noah's Ark" of plant life to Nashville was monumental. Individual trees weighed as much as 16 tons and cost $5,000 to purchase and ship. In the end, 32 tractor-trailers were required to deliver all of the Delta's tropical flora.

The big day for the opening of Phase IV finally arrived. An editorial in a Nashville newspaper of June 6, 1996, declared the Delta would be "a major asset for the community and a significant contributor to the local economy." The editorial went on to describe the attraction:

> The Delta is a 4.5-acre construction encompassing an indoor garden area, almost 1,000 new guest rooms, 20 new meeting rooms, a giant 1.25-acre ballroom and more exhibit space for conventions and trade shows. Three years and $175 million in the building, it makes Opryland the largest combined hotel/convention center under one roof anywhere. . . .
>
> The Delta carries a decided subtropical flavor, thanks to palm trees, New Orleans-style buildings, a West Indian mahogany tree,

Just as Swensson predicted, people enjoy themselves — lunching, meeting, strolling, sitting on the balconies of their rooms — with a view of botanical exotica from Africa, India and Japan, as well as homegrown beauties, such as Southern live oaks, magnolia trees, azaleas and rhododendron.

Soon after the Conservatory opened, Swensson walked into the garden to conduct an informal survey and spotted a couple sitting on a bench. The architect asked if they were Opryland guests. "Oh no," they said, "We're from McMinnville (Tennessee, 60 miles away.). We come down here on Sunday afternoons to relax."

McMinnville, Swensson notes, is nationally known as a flower capital. "If the Opryland garden drew McMinnville residents," he said, "I knew we had succeeded."

> magnolias and unusual swamp/bayou type plants. Rooms overlooking the gardens have individual balconies. An indoor river stretches more than a quarter-mile and will be equipped with flatboats that carry passengers on a 10-minute pleasure cruise. There are two waterfalls and a fountain with jets that shoot water 85 feet up toward the Delta Dome.

For convention planners, the Delta's outstanding attraction was the new ballroom. With a seating capacity of 5,000, the cavernous, 55,000-square-foot space was almost twice as large as a football field and could accommodate a variety of configurations for banquet- or theater-style seating. One Nashville reporter, after viewing the huge ballroom, quipped that it could hold more people than the populations of many of Tennessee's smaller cities and towns. The Opryland Hotel now housed the four largest ballrooms in Tennessee.

1 9 9 7

In the spring of 1997, Bud Wendell retired as president and chief executive officer of Gaylord Entertainment after 47 years with Gaylord and National Life. With a wise and seasoned hand, Wendell had directed the phenomenal success of Gaylord Entertainment attractions, from the hotel, Grand Ole Opry and theme park to

JACK VAUGHN WITH CLOSE ASSOCIATES: (TOP) ARCHITECT EARL SWENSSON, CENTER, AND MARKETER MIKE DIMOND; (MIDDLE) CEO BUD WENDELL AND CORPO-RATE SALES DIRECTOR MARGARET PARKER; (BOTTOM) MANAGER JOE HENRY.

television stations and the Ryman Auditorium restoration. In recognition of his leadership, the company's brick headquarters on Briley Parkway had been dedicated in 1995 as the "E.W. Wendell Building." Jack Vaughn hailed Wendell as "one of the premier managers of the 20th century."

Filling Wendell's shoes in May 1997 as Gaylord Entertainment Company president and CEO was Terry

London. A CPA and an Oklahoma native who once played basketball under legendary coach Hank Iba at Oklahoma State, London had been with Gaylord Entertainment and its related companies since 1978, rising to chief financial officer of the conglomerate. Most recently, he had served as its executive vice president and chief operating officer.

For Gaylord Entertainment, change was in the air. The company, which boasted annual revenues of $500 million and assets of over $1 billion, decided to emphasize the lodging portion of its multi-faceted business ventures, and London began streamlining operations. Only recently, the company had announced it would sell two of its Nashville-based holdings, The Nashville Network (TNN) and Country Music Television (CMT).

> *"Where else can you find a hotel with the kind of atmosphere we have along with the meeting space. That's why we have recognition among meeting planners of well over 80 percent."*
>
> —David Jones

By mid-summer 1997, London and his Gaylord team were exploring options for the Opryland Park site and in early November announced that the park would be replaced by a giant, $200 million retail and entertainment mall called Opry Mills. Projections called for 200 stores and restaurants in the 1.2-million-square-foot development.

Intent on duplicating Opryland Hotel's formula for success, Gaylord Entertainment officials announced in January 1998 that a second Opryland Hotel would be built near Orlando, Florida, as part of a one-billion-dollar entertainment complex next to Walt Disney World. Designed around a giant, indoor Caribbean garden, the new hotel would intially contain 1,400 guest rooms, a 200,000-square-foot exhibit hall and

GAYLORD ENTERTAINMENT COMPANY PRESIDENT TERRY LONDON, FRONT LEFT; OPRYLAND HOSPITALITY GROUP PRESIDENT DAVID JONES, FRONT RIGHT; OPRYLAND HOTEL AND ATTRACTIONS PRESIDENT JACK GAINES, FRONT CENTER; HOTEL MANAGER AND VICE PRESIDENT RAY WATERS, REAR LEFT; GENERAL MANAGER AND SENIOR VICE PRESIDENT JOE HENRY, REAR RIGHT.

150,000 square feet of meeting space, at a total investment of $300 million.

To assure success of its hotel properties, Gaylord Entertainment formed the Opryland Hospitality Group in early 1998 and named Jack Vaughn, then president of Opryland Hotel and Attractions Group, as chairman. When Vaughn retired from the post several months later to serve as consultant to the Opryland Hospitality Group, David Jones, a veteran hotelier, became the group's president and CEO. Jones had served the previous five years as president and chief operating officer of John Q. Hammons Hotels Inc., where he oversaw development of 16 new properties for the hotel chain and led the company through its initial public offering.

Jack Gaines, a 30-year veteran of the hospitality business, was named president of Opryland Hotel and Attractions. Like his friend, Jack Vaughn, Gaines had worked for Westin Hotels and Resorts in a number of posts that included following Vaughn as general manager of the Westin Hotel in Chicago. Gaines held the title of Westin's senior vice president before joining Omni Hotels as senior vice president and director of operations and then establishing his own hotel consulting business, where he had occasion to work with the Opryland Hotel. When he was named president, the hotel welcomed not only a highly regarded professional but a friend.

Providing continuity at Opryland Hotel amid changes in personnel was senior vice president and general manager Joe Henry. The man who had been hired by Vaughn before the hotel was built and who had helped engineer its successful growth and rising reputation for nearly three decades now worked with Gaines to maintain the quality of Gaylord Entertainment's flagship hotel property. Even as the company announced intentions to build and operate several new hotels across the United States, it was clear the original hotel would remain the standard-bearer.

In October 1998, Gaylord Entertainment announced plans for a second, new

The Hotel's
Star Attractions

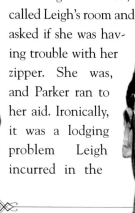

Special occasions regularly bring luminaries from the world of politics, sports, business, the arts and entertainment to the Opryland Hotel. Johnny Cash and Margaret Thatcher, Roy Rogers and Joe DiMaggio, Maya Angelou and Bob Hope and every U.S. president since Jimmy Carter have visited.

The visits, however, don't always go without a hitch. Actress Janet Leigh, who starred in Alfred Hitchcock's classic thriller, "Psycho," was at the hotel for an annual book-and-author dinner. When she didn't appear for the cocktail party preceding the event, program sponsors became worried.

Acting on a hunch, veteran hotel staffer Margaret Parker called Leigh's room and asked if she was having trouble with her zipper. She was, and Parker ran to her aid. Ironically, it was a lodging problem Leigh incurred in the

Opryland Hotel, this one to be built in Grapevine, Texas, north of the Dallas-Fort Worth area. Designed with a "frontier spirit" motif, the hotel was planned to provide 1,500 guest rooms and cost $350 million. To coordinate sales efforts among Gaylord Entertainment's rapidly growing list of hotel properties, a national sales office was organized in February 1999 to assure customers of the Opryland Hotel in Nashville that they would experience the same level of amenities and service in Florida and Texas. Headquarters for the sales group was placed in Nashville, with

movie thriller. Parker didn't mean the question as a joke and asked only to be helpful.

Parker also came to the rescue of Roy Rogers, the beloved King of the Cowboys, who was a guest at the hotel while taking part in a County Music Association Awards show. When Rogers appeared in the lobby, fans started surging toward him.

Parker, who was escorting him to the entrance of the hotel, brought the stampede to a

LEFT: PRESIDENT NIXON RECEIVED A YO-YO LESSON FROM ROY ACUFF AT THE NEWLY OPENED OPRY HOUSE IN 1974.

RIGHT: GEORGE AND BARBARA BUSH CELEBRATED THEIR 50TH WEDDING ANNIVERSARY AT THE HOTEL IN 1995, HERE GREETED BY SPECIAL PROMOTIONS DIRECTOR SANDY STUCKEY.

subsidiary offices located in Chicago and Washington, D. C.

"We can take the Opryland concept and recreate it to fit the local market," Jones declared in an interview in *Lodging,* the management magazine of the American Hotel and Motel Association. He explained Opryland's unique appeal: "Where else can you find a hotel with the kind of atmosphere we have along with that meeting space. That is why we have recognition among meeting planners of well over 80 percent."

2 0 0 0

Compared to other great American hotels—the Grand Hotel at Mackinac Island in Michigan, the Broadmoor at Colorado Springs, the Willard in Washington, D.C., or the Plaza in New York City, for example—the Opryland Hotel is the new kid on the block. It has far to go to reach its half-century mark, certainly not venerable by hotel industry standards.

Yet, though a youngster, the Opryland Hotel has achieved more fame and

---

halt with a brief but firm speech. "I told them there would be no autographs and only one picture," she recalls. The fans and Rogers obliged. Impressed, Rogers offered to take the efficient staffer on the road with him.

When Presidents and former Presidents arrive, they bring a retinue of Secret Service agents. Staff-only corridors are inspected and guarded so safe, non-public entrances and exits are available. The advance work of agents reached a pitch when President Bill Clinton and Vice President Albert Gore appeared together at the hotel in 1997.

Huge country music fans, former President and First Lady George and Barbara Bush checked into the hotel in 1995 to celebrate their 50th wedding anniversary. Event coordinator Sandy Stuckey handled myriad details, even

finding a way to duplicate their wedding cake.

Roy Acuff's 81st birthday brought sitting President Ronald Reagan to Opryland as a guest for the Grand Ole Opry House event in 1984. When the President and Acuff walked on stage, they faced a five-foot-tall plaster cake hauled out on such occasions. For the ceremonial cutting, a slice of the plaster had been sawed out and real cake and icing placed inside.

Reagan may have been "The Great Communicator," but it was Acuff's remarks that sent the audience into gales of laughter that night. He told Reagan, "Cut it here. The rest is plaster!" The fake-cake secret, revealed by Acuff not in a stage whisper but over the microphone, triggered a sea of waving American flags and blizzard of confetti. ▨

---

success than establishments many times its age. It has been blessed by the creativity and guidance of people of vision who demanded that it become one of the finest hotels in America. And, from its beginnings, it has been supported by a staff of thousands of men and women—secretaries to computer programmers, bellhops to horticulturists, chefs and wait staff to laundry workers—who were, and are, satisfied with nothing less than excellence in their day-to-day duties.

Like most popular resorts, the Opryland Hotel has hosted many of the world's rich and famous. Richard Nixon, Gerald Ford, Ronald Reagan, George Bush and Bill Clinton, either as presidents of the United States or as former presidents, have been guests at Opryland. Other national figures such as Generals Norman Schwarzkopf and Colin Powell, Ross Perot, Steve Forbes, Al Gore and Bob Dole have stayed at the hotel. Hollywood celebrities Mickey Rooney, Bob Hope, Lauren Bacall and Lassie have visited, as well as best-selling novelist Irving Stone, business magnate Lee Iococca, and sports heroes Joe DiMaggio and Johnny Unitas.

Virtually every kind of gathering has been held at the hotel. Societies and associations of engineers, casket makers, travel agents, publishers and booksellers, social scientists, elk hunters, and computer software vendors are among the groups made to feel at home in Opryland's facilities.

As the hotel has grown in number of guest rooms and size of banquet halls, meeting rooms and exhibit space, so has the scale of organizations eager to book conven-

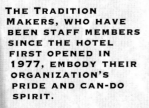

THE TRADITION MAKERS, WHO HAVE BEEN STAFF MEMBERS SINCE THE HOTEL FIRST OPENED IN 1977, EMBODY THEIR ORGANIZATION'S PRIDE AND CAN-DO SPIRIT.

tions. Today, with nearly 3,000 guest rooms, meeting spaces of every size and configuration, hundreds of thousands of square feet of exhibit halls, and a state-of-the-art, fiber-optics communications system capable of handling the most advanced and complex electronic requirements, the Opryland Hotel can accommodate virtually any convention in North America.

Since opening in 1977, the hotel has expanded three times while maintaining an occupancy rate of more than 80 percent. Its 600,000 square feet of meeting space, its nine acres of shops, and its streams and gardened walkways under glass canopies make it unique in the world. Once a visitor arrives at the hotel, there's

Known by the Companies We Keep

On any given day within the Opryland Hotel's 600,000 square feet of meeting space, a dozen organizations are holding conventions. For the likes of Coca-Cola and IBM, American Bar and American Medical associations, Burger King and BellSouth, the Opryland Hotel is a favorite venue. "We make sure every meeting excels," says sales executive Jerry Wayne.

The logistics of feeding, entertaining and lodging large groups is a challenge. For a National Chiefs of Police gathering, the hotel staff fed 5,000 attendees while the remaining 5,000 were ushered to a performance of the Grand Ole Opry. Then the order was reversed, with the Opryland staff given 20 minutes to clean and reset the ballroom for the second seating.

The unusual is the dietary norm. When 6,000 people from India attended a convention at Opryland, the hotel's

no reason to brave the elements the rest of the stay. It is a concept that works to perfection and will be taken to other major convention markets in the nation.

At a tribute dinner for Jack Vaughn in March 1999, reminiscences flowed like wine. Rex Holmes was the 7 a.m. doorman on the hotel's opening day in November 1977, and he recalled that everything seemed in perfect readiness. "Here comes Mr. Vaughn," Holmes said. "As I usher him in and begin walking back to the entrance, he turns and says, 'Young man, did you notice that the third lightbulb on the right of the flagpole is not working?'" Added Homes admiringly: "What a man for detail."

The account was vintage Jack Vaughn. His passion for excellence and his mind for innovation, taking the concept of a convention-center-within-a-hotel to new heights, spelled unprecedented success for the Opryland Hotel. In little more than 20 years, the hotel had become a legend in the hospitality industry. David Jones, president of the Opryland Hospitality Group, said this explains why the great hotel companies in the nation as well as the American Hotel and Motel Association repeatedly book conventions at the hotel. They want to inspire their own people by letting them experience the best.

It had been a few short decades since Irving Waugh walked into Val

culinary staff took a quick course in Indian cuisine. At a convention during the month of Ramadan, Moslem attendees stood silently at the head of the buffet tables until a bell rang signaling the day's fast was over and the festivities could begin. At a lively gypsy wedding in the Tennessee Ballroom, a whole roasted pig was on the menu.

Conventions bring their own flavor to the hotel. At meetings of Rotary International, participants have worn native garb while flags of their countries were flown from the hotel entrance, creating the trappings of a multi-ethnic city. At a meeting of the National Conference of Christians and Jews, Jack Vaughn showcased the diversity of the hotel's

Smith's office in 1968 with a concept for a park and a hotel to serve it. In the nine-year gestation period that preceded the birth of the Opryland Hotel, magic thinking had occurred. A general manager had been hired who showered ideas like Chinese rockets, and he had been privileged to work with an architect and a marketer and a second-in-command who were second to none. Giving them the chance to try their ideas were the open-minded management teams of National Life and Gaylord Entertainment, and making the concept work on the floor was a staff that believed in the philosophy of day-to-day excellence.

The future looks as bright as the past for the Opryland Hotel and its parent company, Gaylord Entertainment. New Opryland Hotels will bring Opryland's total dining-shopping-conventioneering-entertainment experience to other markets. "Bud Wendell laid the foundation," said Jack Vaughn. "Now, Terry London is going to take this brand new (Gaylord) team and grow the company faster and larger and smarter than Wall Street ever imagined."

Gaylord Entertainment Company is committed to doing just that, while safeguarding the traditions it inherits and oversees. According to London, Gaylord Entertainment regards itself as "caretaker of three valuable franchises:

staff. The gesture was greeted with enthusiastic applause.

Large conventions feature nationally known speakers and equally well-known mascots. When Exxon employees arrived for a meeting, so did the company symbol, the Exxon tiger, which had to be gingerly transported in a freight elevator for its guest appearance on stage. Taco Bell brought its telegenic chihuahua, and the Air Force Academy's choral group, featured on a Country Music Association awards program, flew in with its falcon.

Able to rival Las Vegas in glitz, Opryland featured fireworks, dancing fountains and daggers of laser light in celebrating the Delta's first anniversary. For a party in the Cascades, Nashville Symphony musicians played from the balconies of rooms facing the garden and the maestro conducted from a platform on the roof of a bar.

Perhaps the highest compliment paid Opryland Hotel's accommodations came from the world's largest hospitality organization, the American Hotel & Motel Association, which twice within a decade chose Opryland as its convention site.

Grand Ole Opry and its music tradition, an American institution and art form; Opryland hotel and convention centers; and ventures that celebrate family values." The entire country is the beneficiary of all three.

As president of the hotel, Jack Gaines applauds two organizations that have made it a success. "We recognize the courage of National Life to pursue the initial dream and the faith of Bud Wendell and Jack Vaughn to make it happen," he says. "And we salute the commitment of Gaylord Entertainment to the hotel's growing success. In effect, they have said, 'We're going to make our contribution to this great lady.' And they have."

SAVANNAH-INSPIRED GALLERIA FOUNTAIN, MAGNOLIA LOBBY

RIGHT: FRONT PORCH, OLD HICKORY ROOM

PREVIOUS SPREAD: A TRADITION OF HOSPITALITY

CRYSTAL GAZEBO, CONSERVATORY

RIGHT: GUEST ROOMS, CASCADES

PREVIOUS SPREAD: BRICK MURAL, CASCADES LOBBY ENTRANCE

GUZMANIA BROMELIAD, CASCADES

PREVIOUS SPREAD: WATERFALLS, CASCADES

DELTA MARSH MALLARDS BY SCULPTOR TOM GRISCOM, DELTA

DOORMAN, MAGNOLIA LOBBY

RIGHT: GUEST SAMANTHA SOWELL PLAYING BEFORE A BRUCE MATTHEWS MURAL, "UN APRÈS-MIDI DE DOUCE OISIVETÉ" (AN AFTERNOON OF SWEET LAZINESS), AT DELTA ENTRANCE

MAITRE D' WILLIE NIKOLAICZYK, OLD HICKORY ROOM

RIGHT: VOLARE' RESTAURANT, CONSERVATORY

MANTLE FROM NATIONAL LIFE BUILDING, PRESIDENTIAL SUITE

PREVIOUS SPREAD: PRESIDENTIAL SUITE

CASCADES RESTAURANT, CASCADES

CHEF RICHARD GERST AND SEVERAL MEMBERS OF HIS AWARD-WINNING TEAM

RIGHT: WEDDING CAKE DECORATION

SANDOR MATYI AND ICE CARVING

RIGHT: DANIEL BOURGEOIS, PASTRY CHEF

84

DELTA BALLROOM

RIGHT: SHOW PREPARATION, DELTA BALLROOM

CONVENTION OF MEETING PLANNERS INTERNATIONAL, PRESIDENTIAL BALLROOM

87

Café Avanti, Conservatory

MAGNOLIA BALLROOM FOYER

LEFT: MAGNOLIA BALLROOM

DELTA RIVER

RIGHT: DELTA OVERVIEW

DELTA FOUNTAIN

RIGHT: FRENCH QUARTER, DELTA

INSPIRATIONS GIFT SHOP, MAGNOLIA LOBBY

AUNT PITTY PAT'S DOLL SHOP

FOLLOWING SPREAD: DELTA CROWDS

"SATURDAY NIGHT" BY WAYLAND MOORE, PICKIN' PARLOR LOUNGE ENTRANCE

LEFT: JUNE CARTER CASH INTERVIEWED BY KEITH BILBREY IN WSM RADIO STUDIO, MAGNOLIA LOBBY

ENTRANCE, RUSTY'S SPORTS BAR

VENDOR IN FRONT OF RUSTY'S SPORTS BAR MURAL, "THE LEGENDS," BY ROY BELL.

ANTIQUE STAINED GLASS CEILING, PICKIN' PARLOR

VINTAGE FRENCH POSTER, PICKIN' PARLOR SALOON

GENERAL JACKSON RIVERBOAT, CUMBERLAND RIVER

PREVIOUS SPREAD: REFLECTION, GENERAL JACKSON

Musical production, General Jackson stage

WILDHORSE SALOON, SECOND AVENUE SOUTH, NASHVILLE

WILDHORSE SALOON

BACKSTAGE AT THE OPRY

LEFT: ON STAGE, GRAND OLE OPRY

THE LATE ROY ACUFF IN HIS DRESSING ROOM AT THE OPRY HOUSE

Opryland Hotel · Nashville

PREVIOUS SPREAD: A NIGHT AT THE OPRY HOUSE

THE LATE MINNIE PEARL BACKSTAGE AT GRAND OLE OPRY

118

DISPLAYS AT GRAND OLE OPRY MUSEUM

RIGHT: MARTY ROBBINS' COAT, GRAND OLE OPRY MUSEUM

PREVIOUS SPREAD: MINNIE PEARL'S HAT, GRAND OLE OPRY MUSEUM

GRAND OLE OPRY MUSEUM

RIGHT: WAX FIGURE OF LITTLE JIMMY DICKENS, GRAND OLE OPRY MUSEUM

RYMAN AUDITORIUM IN NASHVILLE LOBBY MURAL BY T. MAX HOCHSTETLER

RIGHT: SIMULATED OPRY STAGE EXPERIENCE, GRAND OLE OPRY MUSEUM

126

ORIGINAL SPRINGHOUSE, SPRINGHOUSE GOLF COURSE

PREVIOUS SPREAD: SPRINGHOUSE GOLF CLUB

127

SPRINGHOUSE GOLF COURSE

18TH GREEN, SPRINGHOUSE GOLF COURSE

PREVIOUS SPREAD: SPRINGHOUSE GOLF COURSE

BELLSOUTH SENIOR CLASSIC ON PGA SENIOR TOUR, SPRINGHOUSE GOLF CLUB

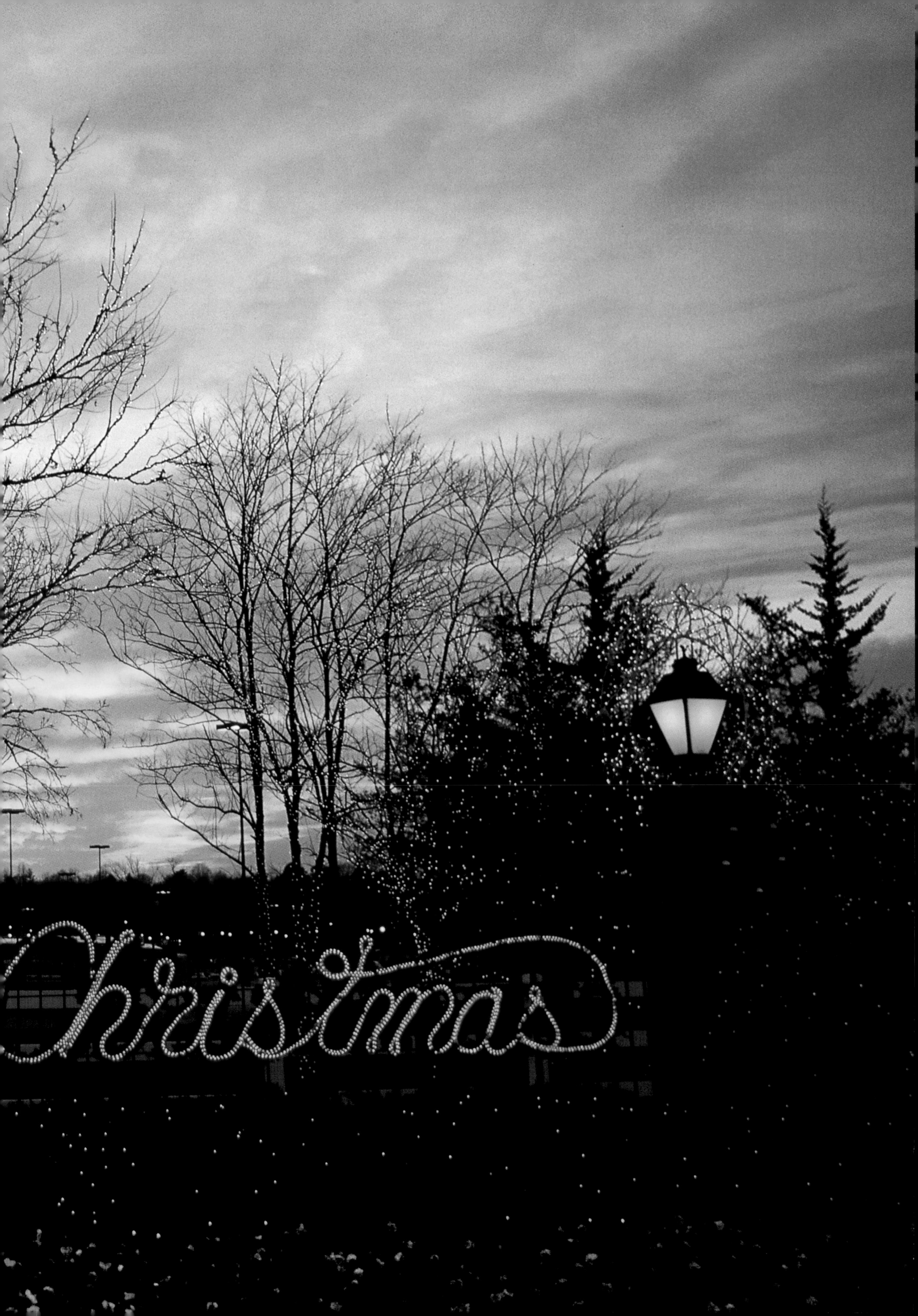
Christmas

SANTA, PRESIDENTIAL LOBBY

PREVIOUS SPREAD: OPRYLAND HOTEL ENTRY DRIVE, CHRISTMAS SEASON

TRAIN EXHIBIT, MAGNOLIA LOBBY

FOLLOWING SPREAD: GALLERIA FOUNTAIN, MAGNOLIA LOBBY

ENTRANCE TO DELTA

LEFT: CAFÉ AVANTI, CONSERVATORY

CONSERVATORY

LEFT: CONSERVATORY

142

OPRYLAND HOTEL ENTRY DRIVE

NATIVITY SCENE, VERANDA REFLECTING POOL

GINGERBREAD VILLAGE, DELTA BALLROOM LOBBY

PREVIOUS SPREAD: DELTA

CHEF RICHARD GERST AND CHRISTMAS BUFFET, DELTA BALLROOM

FOLLOWING SPREAD: TAPING RAY STEVENS IN A CBS HOLIDAY SPECIAL, DELTA

152

CHRISTMAS MORNING, MAGNOLIA ENTRANCE

PREVIOUS SPREAD: ENTRY DRIVE GATEHOUSE